LAND
UNDER
THE
SEA

A SKYLIGHT BOOK

LAND UNDER THE SEA

Hershell H. Nixon
and
Joan Lowery Nixon

Illustrated with photographs

DODD, MEAD & COMPANY • NEW YORK

PICTURE CREDITS

Courtesy of The Cousteau Society, Inc., 930 W. 21st Street, Norfolk, VA 23517, a membership supported environmental organization, page 42; Scripps Institution of Oceanography, 17, 18, 19, 20, 21, 24, 37, 38; Office of Learning Resources, Scripps Institution of Oceanography, 52; from Marie Tharp's world ocean floor panorama, 8, 14, 32, 34, 51; Woods Hole Oceanographic Institution, 11, 15, 25, 28, 45, 47, 48, 49, 57; Woods Hole Oceanographic Institution, by Robert Ballard, 54, by Rod Catanach, 22 (bottom), by Vicky Cullen, 59, by Larry Workman, 22 (top).

Library of Congress Cataloging in Publication Data

Nixon, Hershell H.
    Land under the sea.

    (A Skylight book)
    Includes index.
    Summary: Describes the exploration of the land
beneath the sea and what it has revealed about the
topography of this vast hidden area. Also discusses how
these discoveries help us better understand the earth
upon which we live.
    1. Underwater exploration—Juvenile literature.
2. Submarine topography—Juvenile literature.
[1. Underwater exploration.   2. Submarine topography]
I. Nixon, Joan Lowery.   II. Title.
GC65.N58 1985   910.09162   85-7041
ISBN 0-396-08582-2

For Michael Joseph Quinlan
with our love

ACKNOWLEDGMENTS

With gratitude for their kind assistance to: Public Affairs Representative
Charles R. Colgan, Dr. Peter Lonsdale, and Cmdr. Skip Theberge, Scripps
Institution of Oceanography; Public Information Director Shelley Luzon,
Dr. Hans Schouten, and Dr. Jeffrey A. Karson, Woods Hole Oceanographic
Institution.

Charts of the world ocean floor panorama are available
in several sizes from Marie Tharp, One Washington Av-
enue, South Nyack, New York 10960, U.S.A.

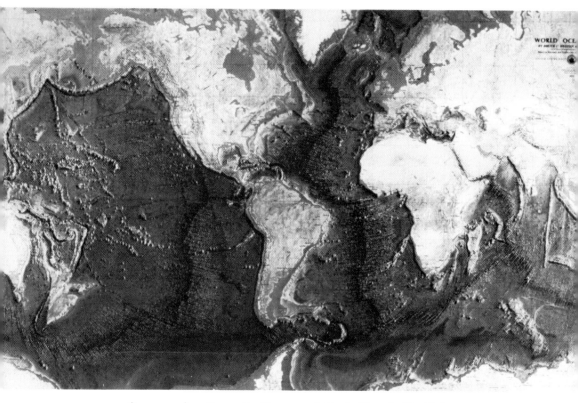

Oceanographers Bruce C. Heezen and Marie Tharp's World Ocean Floor Panorama, the first complete map of what was charted and what was thought to be found on the sea floors around the world.

The immense oceans which separate the continents of the world have long been a source of power, of awesome beauty, and of mystery. Spreading over three-quarters of the surface of the earth, since time began they have hidden the secret land that lies beneath them.

But for many years *oceanographers*, explorers of the sea, have hunted for ways to learn about this unexplored land so that we might better understand the earth upon which we live.

As new tools and instruments were invented, oceanographers learned to use some of them to aid their own studies. Bit by bit they made exciting discoveries: canyons deeper than any canyons known on dry land, volcanoes erupting molten lava and minerals into the water, gigantic plains which rise into mountains and huge mountain ranges, and a sea floor that continues to spread, rolling under or pushing upward.

EARLY EXPLORERS

By studying currents, ocean winds, and sailing charts, some early navigators guessed at what they might find in the shape of the land that lay beneath the waters. Matthew Fontaine Maury, a U.S. Navy officer, was the first to bring together records of wind patterns and currents from thousands of ships' logs, producing sailing charts that aided seamen around the world. In 1855, in his publication *The Physical Geography of the Sea*, he wrote of what he thought must be a "remarkable steppe" in the Mid-Atlantic Ocean. Seventeen years later he was proved to be right.

In 1890 a group of marine scientists went to sea on the British ship, H.M.S. *Challenger*, and spent almost four years studying all aspects of the Atlantic, Pacific, and

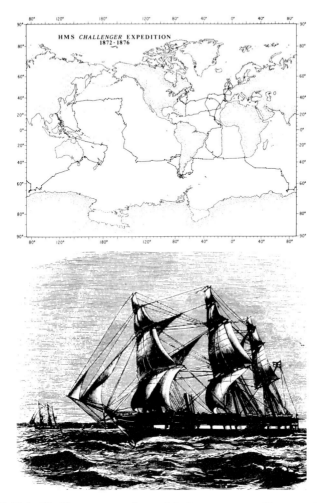

The H.M.S. Challenger *was the world's first oceanographic research ship. She was fitted with steam power in addition to her sails. In three-and-a-half years the ship sailed 8,890 miles, doing research in all oceans except the Arctic.*

11

"southern" oceans. Water temperature readings that varied made them think there could be a high mountain ridge, or barrier, that divided the Atlantic Ocean.

World War I interrupted scientific exploration of the oceans, and little was done until after World War II. By this time equipment had been invented which could be used to take measurements and record a pattern of the land under the sea. And there were submarines which could take scientists right down to the ocean floor. Studies had been made which proved the early explorers on the H.M.S. *Challenger* had been right about a high mountain ridge that divided the floor of the Atlantic Ocean. This ridge was named the Mid-Atlantic Ridge.

In 1947 geophysicist Maurice Ewing and geology students Bruce Heezen and Frank Press went to sea in *The Atlantis*, a ship from the Woods Hole Oceanographic Institution in Massachusetts. Their project was to learn more about the floor of the Atlantic Ocean around the Mid-Atlantic Ridge.

Using a depth finder, which bounces sound waves off the ocean floor, they discovered a wide plain, called an *abyssal plain*, which was as smooth as mud. Then they came to what seemed to be foothills. Finally they found themselves over a huge area of very tall, rugged mountains which were broken by canyons and deep valleys: the Mid-Atlantic Ridge.

At the Lamont-Doherty Geological Observatory at Columbia University in Palisades, New York, Bruce Heezen began mapping the floors of the world's oceans with the help of his assistant, oceanographer Marie Tharp. Sounding equipment was used on ships to help them navigate harbors, but Tharp requested captains of all seagoing ships to keep using their sounding equipment as they traveled across the oceans. She and Heezen gathered increasingly more accurate depth recordings and echo-soundings from oceanographic centers around the world and used this information to construct a panorama of the ocean floor, which was drawn in three dimensions.

As they developed their maps of the world's oceans, exciting pieces of information began to appear.

They found that the Mid-Atlantic Ridge, which lies in a north-south direction, is only a part of a mid-ocean

The Mid-Ocean Ridge runs down the middle of the Atlantic Ocean. In the Pacific Ocean it is on the eastern side. The Mid-Atlantic Ridge is offset by fracture zones in a shape similar to the African bulge. Iceland is an island which was created by volcanic activity along the ridge.

14

chain of mountains which are 40,000 miles long (60,000 kilometers). This chain wraps around the world, winding in different directions through every ocean. "Like the seams on a baseball," Tharp said. Heezen called this chain the Mid-Ocean Ridge, and it covers as much of the earth's surface as all of the continents put together.

Tharp saw that deep, V-shaped valleys seemed to run along the crest of the mountains in the ridges. At the same time, areas of current earthquakes were being mapped, as were areas of past earthquakes through the records they left of fissures and movement of rocks. Hee-

This fissure in the rocks was discovered on the Mid-Atlantic Ridge.

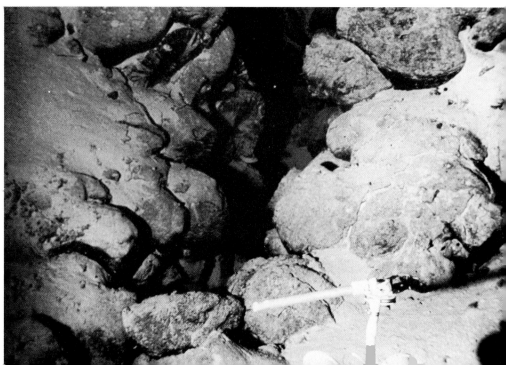

zen discovered that many of the underwater earthquakes and volcanic eruptions had taken—and were taking place—along these valleys. The mountain ranges in the Mid-Ocean Ridge were in an active process of changing and growing.

Many more ocean expeditions were made from oceanographic centers around the world. And as more and more information was gathered and shared, a picture began to take shape of another world that lay beneath the seas.

THE OCEANOGRAPHERS' TOOLS

Early soundings were made by dropping explosive depth charges of dynamite to the ocean floor and measuring the sound waves that bounced back. But today electronic echo-soundings are made by systems such as Sea Beam, which is installed on the ship *R.V. Thomas Washington* and operated by Scripps Institution of Oceanography. Instead of using a single sonar beam, it bounces 16 beams against the sea floor, covering an area up to a mile wide on each side of the ship's track. The echo signals are sent to a computer on the ship and recorded on paper in a 11-

16

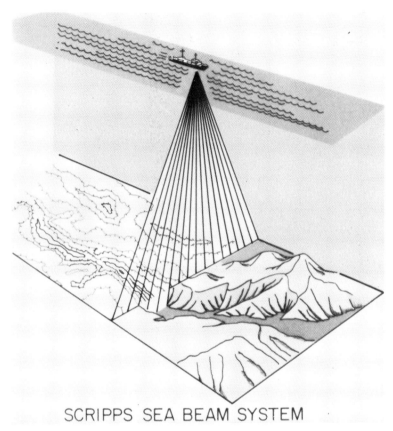

SCRIPPS SEA BEAM SYSTEM

Sea Beam sends out sixteen echo sounder beams across an invisible track at right angles to the ship's track. In this way an area up to a mile on each side of the ship's track can be plotted.

inch-wide chart. The shape of the sea floor can be drawn along the entire track of the ship.

Sonar, which transmits high-frequency sound in a nar-

17

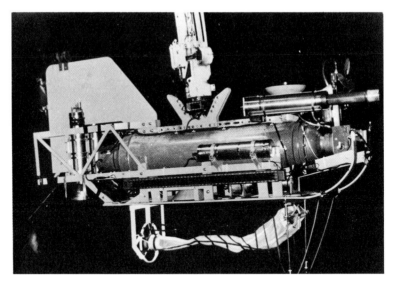

Deep Tow, *which was developed by the Marine Physical Laboratory at the Scripps Institution of Oceanography, can be towed underwater by a ship. It has many uses, such as taking photographs, making echo soundings, and taking water temperature samples.*

row beam into the interior of the sea, is used to make a detailed map of wide areas of the sea floor. GLORIA, which stands for Geological Long-Range Inclined ASDIC (The British name for sonar), is a side-scan sonar which is towed 165 feet (50 meters) underwater by a research ship. GLORIA reflects sound pulses off the sea floor and can map sections up to 38 miles wide (60 kilometers).

Deep Tow is a system that can also be towed underwater by a ship. It can be lowered to 20,000 feet. It is a combination of echo sounder, subbottom sounder, side-looking sonar, stereo cameras, and slow-scan TV with strobe lights. Among these and other functions, it can also measure water temperature and test for minerals suspended in the water.

The *Glomar Challenger* is equipped with tools that can drill into the sea floor and bring up core samples of the rock. Over the past few years, a number of ocean-drilling programs have been carried out with the *Glomar Chal-*

Dr. Peter F. Lonsdale, at Scripps Institution of Oceanography, compares a Sea Beam *chart with sea floor profiles collected by Scripps'* Deep Tow *system.*

The Glomar Challenger, *operated by Scripps Institution of Oceanography, University of California, San Diego, drills and cores for ocean sediment in all the oceans of the world.*

20

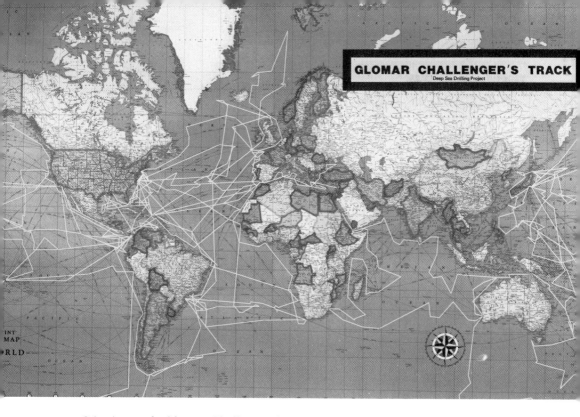

Scientists on the Glomar Challenger *have taken core samples from the sea floor in oceans around the world.*

lenger. Some have been sponsored by JOI, which is the Joint Oceanographic Institutions, a group of ten academic oceanographic institutions in the United States. In some of the programs, JOI has been joined by oceanographic organizations in Germany, France, Japan, Great Britain, and Russia.

A favorite tool of oceanographers is the small sub-

21

The research ship Atlantis II *is the mother ship for* Alvin. *It carries the small submarine to an area to be explored and lowers it to the water so that it can descend to the sea floor.*

Alvin, *the three-man submarine operated by Woods Hole Oceanographic Institution, has been used to study sea floors in many parts of the world. The black smokers and deep sea mineral deposits would not have been found without* Alvin.

marine that allows them to directly study the ocean floor. The French have the *Cyana*, which holds three people and can descend to 9,800 feet (2,987 meters), and the United States has the *Alvin*, which also holds a crew of three and can reach a depth of 13,000 feet (3,962 meters).

Alvin, which has been in service since 1964, is carried on a mother ship, *The Atlantis II*, and is headquartered at Woods Hole Oceanographic Institution. This little battery-powered submarine is 22 feet long (7.62 meters), with a circular space for the crew that is only 7 feet in diameter (2.13 meters). *Alvin* is outfitted with stereo cameras, television cameras, strobe lights, computers, and various measuring devices. It has a remote-controlled arm and claw that can be used to pick up samples from the sea floor and place them in containers on the outside of the submarine.

Through their studies, scientists have made many exciting discoveries.

THE AGE OF THE SEA FLOOR

In 1968 oceanographers in a ship designed for deep-sea drilling, the *Glomar Challenger*, named for the H.M.S.

Men aboard the Glomar Challenger *prepare to drill into the sea floor during the Deep Sea Drilling Project, which was sponsored by oceanographic institutions throughout the United States, France, Germany, Great Britain, Japan, and Russia.*

24

Challenger, began a project to study the sea floor in water so deep it had previously been impossible to get drilling equipment from a ship into the sea floor. By identifying the fossils, type of rock, and composition of rock in the cores drilled by the *Glomar Challenger*, scientists discovered that none of the samples from the ocean floor is older than 200 million years, while rock samples on dry land have tested to be between 3 and 4 billion years old. Determining the age of rocks is usually done through radioactivity tests.

Scientists know that not all parts of the crust of the earth are the same age. Even land under the oceans is not the same age. Samples from the Pacific Ocean are of

Cores of rock taken from many places on the sea floor show oceanographers the types and ages of rock. They have learned about sea floor spreading, ocean floor currents, and volcanic activity on the sea floor through these cores.

younger rock than samples from the Atlantic Ocean, which leads us to believe that the Pacific Ocean was formed after the Atlantic Ocean. And much of the dry land on earth, from deserts to mountains, was long ago under ocean water. This is proved by the many fossils of shells and fish found in these rocks.

To learn more about the sea floor, oceanographers examine former sea floors that are now on land. Dr. Jeffrey A. Karson, at Woods Hole Oceanographic Institution, studies ancient ocean floors that are now exposed in mountain ranges. In walking across the Appalachian Mountains he can go from an area that long ago was a sea floor to rocks that were once in the mantle. He says he can easily spot a place where two continents once crashed together, thrusting the mantle upward.

Based on many tests they have made, scientists think that the inner core of the earth is solid, but around it is an outer core that is liquid. Above and around this outer core is a layer called mantle. The bottom part of this mantle is more solid than the liquid core beneath it, but is still somewhat fluid. The top part of the mantle, where it meets the crust of the earth, is more rigid. The thin, outer crust of the earth is solid. The crust of the earth and the top part of the mantle have been named the *lithosphere*. The crust is thought to be thicker on dry land, about 24 miles deep (35 kilometers), and thinner under the seas, about 3½ miles deep (6 kilometers).

Moving Seaward from Shore

The shoreline is the place where ocean water meets dry land. The shoreline can be softly sloping, sandy beaches. It can be jagged cliffs, or grassy swamps, or quiet ponds, or estuaries—where a river meets the sea. The shoreline can quickly change during a storm, as heavy waves cut away huge chunks of land. And it can change slowly over many years, as sand, gravel, and mud (sediments) are added to the shore.

The Continental Shelf

Continents do not end at the shoreline. They extend outward, under the water, in an almost flat "shelf," or terrace. The widths of these shelves vary greatly, but the

Shoreline

Continental Shelf

Continental
Slope

Continental
Rise

A model at Woods Hole Oceanographic Institution shows features in the continental shelf and the continental slope.

average width is around 47 miles (75 kilometers).

Waves, which cut away at the shoreline, create these shelves. And rocks, gravel, sand, and mud are carried by rivers to the sea and added to the shelves, sometimes extending far out into the ocean in the shape of *fans*. These fans are also called *deltas* or *submarine cones*.

Sediments from the Mississippi River have created a

28

submarine cone so large that it extends from Texas to Alabama across the Gulf of Mexico.

THE CONTINENTAL SLOPE

The continental shelf ends suddenly at the continental slope. This change is called a *shelf break*. The continental slope is much steeper than the shelf slope. It marks the boundary between the continent and the ocean basin.

In some places along the shelf there are deep, wide scars. These are extensions of the rivers which flow into the sea, and are called *submarine canyons*. During the ice ages, when great quantities of ocean water were frozen, the level of the seas dropped, and these canyons were exposed, serving as rivers which led to the sea. So now they are "submarine," or "drowned" rivers.

Many of them are shaped like the Grand Canyon. Some are even larger than this famous canyon, cutting across the entire continental shelf. Just as the Grand Canyon is still being carved by the Colorado River, these submarine canyons are carved by strong, violent currents which carry sudden avalanches of rock, sand, mud, and gravel from the continental shelf out to the continental slope and even to the ocean basins beyond.

The Congo Submarine Canyon, on the west coast of Africa, is the largest canyon that has been discovered. Since it goes from the mouth of the large Congo River across the continental shelf and continental slope, all the material from the Congo River is carried to the floor of the Angola Ocean basin, which lies off the west-central coast of Africa.

In many places the sediment, which is carried into the oceans by currents in the submarine canyons, has created long slopes from the continental shelf into the ocean basin. These slopes are called *continental rise*. These rises are found along the countries bordering the Atlantic Ocean, and are scarce along those bordering the Pacific Ocean, where deep *trenches* are found. Scientists think that the sediments pouring into the Pacific Ocean may be disappearing, through these trenches, into the earth's interior. The Pacific Ocean is younger, based on the tests made of rock samples, with more volcanic activity than the Atlantic Ocean. This may be why there are many trenches in the Pacific Ocean and only a few in the Atlantic Ocean. Scientists do not yet know why this is so.

OCEAN TRENCHES

Most ocean trenches are found near the land, along the borders of the Pacific Ocean. They are the deepest part of the ocean, about 5 to 6 ½ miles deep (4 to 5 kilometers). The Mariana Trench, in the South Pacific, is over 36,000 feet deep (11,022 meters). It's deeper than the tallest mountain on earth, Mount Everest in Asia, is high— 29,028 feet (8,848 meters).

The Aleutian Trench, which is located just south of the Alaskan Peninsula, extends from Alaska to the Kamchatka Peninsula in Asia. Trenches have been found in the Atlantic Ocean in the Caribbean area. They are the Puerto Rican and Cayman trenches, which are about 1,200 miles long (1,930 kilometers) in an east-west direction.

Undersea trenches usually range from 30 to 65 miles wide (50 to 100 kilometers), and are thousands of miles long. Many strong earthquakes take place underneath

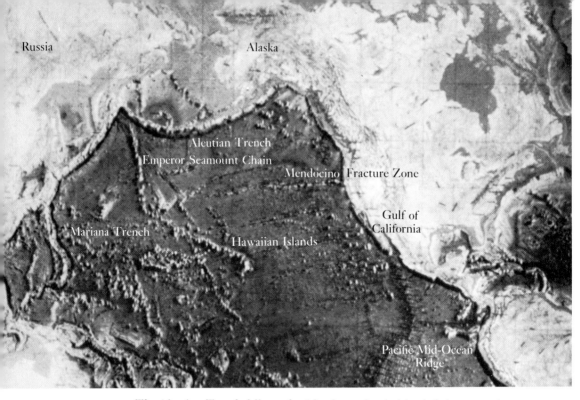

Russia   Alaska

Aleutian Trench
Emperor Seamount Chain
Mendocino Fracture Zone
Gulf of California
Mariana Trench
Hawaiian Islands
Pacific Mid-Ocean Ridge

The Aleutian Trench follows the Aleutian volcanic island chain across the North Pacific from Alaska to Russia. It connects with the Kuril, Japan, and Mariana trenches. The Hawaiian Islands are at the southern end of the Emperor Seamount Chain, which extends northward to the Aleutian Trench. The Mendocino fracture zone, one of the many fracture zones which cross the Mid-Ocean Ridges, reaches from northern California to the Emperor Chain. The Pacific Mid-Ocean Ridge extends into the Gulf of California on the eastern side of the ocean.

these trenches. Volcanoes usually form next to these trenches.

Oceanographers believe that the surface of the world

is divided into eight large areas which "float," moving very, very slowly against each other, on top of the liquid rock in the upper mantle under the crust of the earth. Each of these areas is called a *plate*. The word *tectonic* comes from carpentry, building, and construction. So geologists have teamed it with the word plate to mean a world that is building and constructing itself. They think that the ocean trenches mark the edge of the earth's tectonic plates.

ASEISMIC TROUGHS AND RIDGES

Troughs are as long as trenches, but they are wider and more shallow, and they are called *aseismic*, meaning that they are not areas of earthquake activity. One of the largest, the Emperor Trough in the northern Pacific Ocean, is about 620 miles long (1,000 kilometers), and lies in a northwest-southeast direction.

Aseismic ridges are long submarine mountain ranges that were built by volcanic eruptions long ago, but are no longer sources of activity. An aseismic ridge is the great Ninetyeast Ridge in the Indian Ocean, which was named

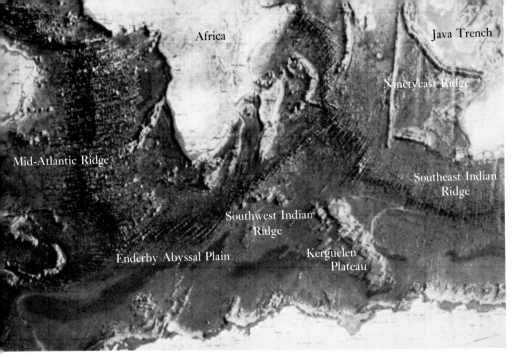

The Mid-Atlantic Ridge meets the Southwest Indian Ridge below the tip of Africa. The Southwest Indian Ridge connects with the Southeast Indian Ridge which extends into the Red Sea. The north-south Ninetyeast Ridge appears to have no fracture zones. To the east of it, the Java Trench curves around Sumatra to the New Guinea islands. A huge submarine plateau, Kerguelen, lies on the east end of the Enderby abyssal plain.

for its location on the longitude line. It is 3,100 miles long (5,000 kilometers).

OCEAN BASINS

More of the surface of the earth is covered by the large ocean basins than by land above the seas. Study of these basins has shown that near the Mid-Ocean Ridge, which runs through all the oceans of the world, the basin floors are rugged. Rock samples taken near the ridge are younger in age than rock that lies closer to shore, since volcanic activity along the ridge pushes rock up and outward. Also, the sediments that cover the floors of the basins are thinner near the Mid-Ocean Ridge and thicker away from the Ridge.

Near the continental rises and slopes are often found widespread, flat areas called *abyssal plains*. One meaning of *abyssal* is: "on the deep ocean floor, where there is no light," and these plains lie in very deep parts of the world's ocean basins. Abyssal plains were probably caused by layer after layer of sediment being washed down upon them in avalanches from the continental shelf. They are much like large mud flats.

Sometimes materials found in the sediment layers have come from very far away, but the currents that carried the rocks and sands and clay were strong enough to sweep them great distances. Sometimes rocks were picked up by glaciers and icebergs and carried thousands of miles before the ice melted and dropped them to the ocean floor. On the plains in the northern part of our oceans, many of these out-of-place rocks, called *glacial erratics*, have been found.

MID-OCEAN CANYONS

There are many strong currents along the ocean floor. They sweep the floor so strongly they have often exposed the bare rock, and they have cut low U-shaped canyons, called mid-ocean canyons. These canyons often connect abyssal plains, carrying sediments from the higher plain to the lower one.

Sometimes the sediments are piled against ridges and undersea mountains in *drifts*, similar to snowdrifts.

PLATEAUS

Scattered throughout the oceans are many mountain-like structures with flat tops and steep sides, called *plateaus*. Their tops were probably worn flat by waves. They usually rise from over half-a-mile to a mile-and-a-half (one to two kilometers) from the sea floor. Some of them are many miles wide and long.

36

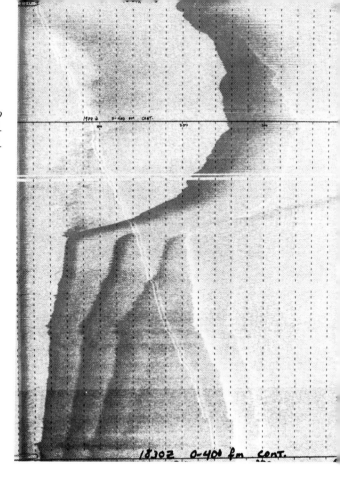

Depth sounders were used to map this plateau, which has an almost vertical side, and its adjoining valley.

There are two kinds of plateaus. Some seem to have been built from volcanic eruptions, while others have the same characteristics of the continents, containing ancient granites. These are called *microcontinents*. Some scientists guess that these could be fragments that have broken off from continents at some time in the past.

37

A depth sounder aboard the Glomar Challenger was used to diagram a seamount.

SEAMOUNTS

There are many, many small hills scattered over the dark ocean floor. These are called *abyssal hills.* But there are mountains which tower over these hills, rising more than 3,000 feet (900 meters) from the floor of the sea. These mountains are called *seamounts,* or the French word, *guyots.* Because their tops have been flattened by wave erosion, they are sometimes called *tablemounts.*

Once they were active volcanoes. Some of them had

38

grown so high they had risen above the water to become islands. But their volcanic activity stopped, which made them stop growing.

Oceanographers have discovered hot spots in the mantle of the earth. As a tectonic plate in the ocean crust slides over a hot spot, a plume of magma sometimes breaks through the crust, erupting into a volcano. As the plate moves away from the hot spot, the volcano is no longer fed with magma and gradually becomes a seamount.

Because these seamounts are heavy, and the crust of the earth is thin where magma had once broken through, they sink very, very slowly into the ocean floor. A large cluster of these seamounts in the Pacific Ocean is called the Mid-Pacific Mountains.

CORAL REEFS AND ATOLLS

Corals are living animals which feed on plankton (tiny animals which live in the ocean) and other organic particles carried by waves in warm ocean waters. A type of algae lives with the corals. The algae's job is to help provide the corals with oxygen and give them the extra energy to take calcium and carbonate ions from the seawater, turning them into a protective wall, or skeleton, which becomes *limestone*. As these skeletons pile and build upon each other, they form *coral reefs*.

Coral reefs begin to grow in the warm, shallow water around the edges of volcanic islands. Some of these volcanoes are no longer fed with magma and become extinct. In the process of becoming seamounts, they begin to sink into the floor of the sea. But as they sink, their coral reefs grow rapidly upward. Finally, after these volcanoes have sunk below the water, only the ring-shaped reefs are left. They protrude above the water, with lagoons in their centers, to form *atolls*. Atolls are found in many places in the South Pacific.

Corals can also grow from the ocean floor in warm, shallow waters. The Great Barrier Reef, off the eastern coast of Australia, stretches 1,250 miles (2,000 kilometers) and is the longest of this type of active, growing coral reef.

Since corals cannot live in cold waters, in deep waters, or on dry land, the changing water levels of the oceans during the ice ages caused many coral reefs to die. Oceanographers have found many older, "drowned" reefs which make up some of the land under the seas.

When the warm, shallow seas subside, then rise again, reefs continue to build upon old reefs, creating limestone banks. The Bahamian Banks grew in this way, creating a chain of islands with beautiful, white limestone sand beaches surrounded by seas that are bright shades of blue.

Within these banks are submarine entrances to caves which contain *stalagmites*. These pillars are found only in caves on dry land, because they are formed by the constant drip of water containing calcium carbonate. So scientists think that these caves were created many, many years ago as rainwater carved them out of the soluble limestone. Now these caves are as deep as 147 feet (45 meters) beneath the surface of the sea. Because the entrances to these caves reflect a deeper blue than the surrounding lighter blue water, they are called *blue holes*.

Stalagmites have been found in blue hole caves at a depth of 148 feet (45 meters). Stalagmites from these caves have been dated, showing they existed in the Ice Age (between 160,000 and 140,000 years ago) when these caves were above sea level. This aerial photograph shows the Cousteau ship, The Calypso, *over one of the blue holes.*

42

The Mid-Ocean Ridge

The Mid-Ocean Ridge is composed of volcanic mountains which have been measured as high as 9,842 feet (3,000 meters) and as wide as 1,243 miles (2,000 kilometers). This mountain ridge winds through every ocean on the earth, and along its crest is a deep valley. The valley is called a *rift*. It's not a peaceful valley. It's the site of frequent, violent earthquakes that measure as high as 7 on the Richter Scale, and constant microearthquakes. While earthquakes that take place on the oceans shelves can set off landslides or cause tidal waves, these Mid-Ocean Ridge earthquakes are so deep beneath the water that they do not disturb the water at the surface of the ocean. But they do make changes in the floor of the ocean.

This rift is also the site where the sea floor breaks open so that molten rock, or *magma*, is pushed upward and out on each side, cooling into lava spills of hard rock. This process is called *sea-floor spreading*.

The Mid-Ocean Ridge is cut by deep right-angle slashes, which extend along the sea floor on both sides of the Ridge. These are called *fracture zones*. In many places

43

between fracture zones the Ridge has moved (has been *offset*) to one side or the other as the floor of the ocean has spread. Some of the large fracture zones have been named. One zone, located between Africa and Brazil, is called Romanche. The Clarion fracture zone extends westward from the tip of Baja California to Hawaii.

Measurements have shown that the tectonic plates of the earth have slowly moved. As magma rises in the valleys of the Mid-Ocean Ridge, it pushes the land on the ocean floor outward. As this land reaches the edges of the ocean plate, sometimes it rolls under the edge of the continental plate. Sometimes two plates collide and push upward, building mountains.

Mountains in the Mid-Ocean Ridge rise above sea level to become dry land in only three places. The Galápagos Islands, located in the Pacific Ocean just off the west coast of Equador; the Azores, which are west of Spain and near the Mid-Atlantic Ridge; and Iceland, in the North Atlantic, are parts of the Mid-Ocean Ridge. It is in Iceland where the Rift Valley, which crosses the island in a north-south direction, is visible on land. Scientists

44

A camera mounted on top of Alvin *looks down into a narrow fissure caused by tectonic activity near the center of the rift valley of the Mid-Atlantic Ridge.*

are able to easily measure the valley with its parallel walls, and they find that it is growing wider.

Oceanographers have discovered seamounts that had

originally formed on ridges, but long ago had split, the two sides carried away from each other by the spreading sea floor.

The ocean floor of the North Atlantic is spreading slowly, only about an inch a year (two centimeters), while the floor in the younger Pacific Ocean, with its greater volcanic activity, is spreading more quickly—as much as six inches a year (16 centimeters). Cores of the ocean floor obtained in studies by scientists aboard *The Glomar Challenger* have shown that during the growth or development of the oceans (200 million years), parts of the sea floor have moved thousands of miles.

UNDERSEA VOLCANOES

Magma erupts from the mantle onto the ocean floor from breaks in the earth's crust along the ridges and trenches, and from other thin or weak spots in the crust of the ocean basins.

In one type of volcanic eruption the magma spills from long cracks or fissures onto the sea floor in what is called *sheet flows*. It is like a shield volcano on land. A shield volcano, such as Kilauea on the island of Hawaii, does not erupt violently. During an eruption, slowly rolling lava flows over its gentle slopes. In another type of underwater eruption the lava rises with more force and builds a volcanic cone.

A sea star seems to guard a cave that was formed by cooling lava during a volcanic eruption on the sea floor. Part of the shell has broken away, creating an entrance to the cave.

One of Alvin's *mechanical arms grabs a sample of pillow lava during a dive on the Mid-Atlantic Ridge.*

Along the Mid-Atlantic Ridge, for example, there are found piles of *pillow lava* which create small hills. These pieces of lava are ridged, which make scientists think that the ridges show cooling stages during which the magma flowed and stopped, then flowed again.

Sometimes the pillow lava takes the shape of long tubes, stretching out onto the ocean floor. Occasionally this is called *toothpaste lava*.

Since H.M.S. *Challenger*'s voyage of discovery, scientists have known that undersea volcanoes are scattered about the ocean basins. But in 1964 Henry W. Menard,

During Project FAMOUS large rolls of "toothpaste lava" were found on the sea floor.

Jr., of the Scripps Institution of Oceanography, made the first thorough study of seamounts in the Pacific Ocean. He found more seamounts in the Pacific than in other oceans, which matched the greater volcanic activity in the Pacific Ocean. Many of these seamounts were found to be in chains that tend to form a line from north to south, with the younger volcanoes at the southern ends. This shows the movement of the Pacific plate to be in a northerly direction.

The Hawaiian Islands make up part of a chain of volcanoes. They are the southwest islands in a chain that is many thousands of miles long. The northern volcanoes no longer reach the surface of the water and have sunk into the crust of the earth, becoming seamounts. The volcanoes in the northern Hawaiian Islands, no longer being fed with magma, are now extinct. The active volcanoes are on the island of Hawaii, which is the southernmost island. A new volcanic island is being formed in the chain, southeast of the island of Hawaii. Even though its top is still about 3,000 feet (914 meters) below the surface of the water, and it will take many, many

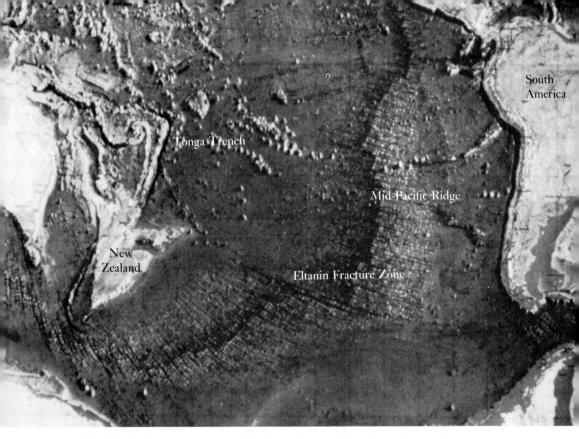

The Eltanin Fracture zone stretches from the tip of South America to the Tonga Trench, north of New Zealand, and offsets the Mid-Pacific Ridge. A deep trench follows the coast of Central and South America. The sea floor is dotted with many seamounts and volcanic islands.

years to appear and become an island, it has been named: *Loihi*.

A chain of undersea volcanoes can be compared to the Cascade Mountains, which is a chain of live volcanoes

51

along the Pacific Coast from Northern California, through Oregon and Washington, into Canada.

In Yellowstone Park we can see different types of volcanic activity. There are geysers and bubbling mud pots, places where heat under the earth's crust is breaking through. And under the sea there are also many types of volcanic activity. Oceanographers have discovered

Dr. James W. Watkins of Scripps Institution of Oceanography, and one of his graduate students, Cynthia A. Evans, study a piece of chimney taken from the top of one of the black smokers found on the East Pacific Rise off Baja California.

"chimneys," vents through which hot, black fluids are pouring into the water from under the crust of the earth. These deep-sea hot springs carry minerals.

In 1978 Project FAMOUS (French-American Mid-Ocean Ridge Undersea Study) conducted a study of sea-floor spreading at the East Pacific Rise, off the coast of Equador. They discovered deposits of manganese, zinc, copper, and silver.

Because of this find, oceanographer Robert D. Ballard became interested in searching for undersea hydrothermal (hot water) activity. In 1979 a research cruise was organized to study the East Pacific Rise off the coast of Mexico. With other American, French, and Mexican scientists, and using the small submarine *Alvin*, Ballard was the first to discover hot-vent chimneys, which were named *black smokers*. These chimneys, near the west coast of Baja California, are long and narrow, rising as high as 65 feet (20 meters), and are only a few feet wide.

Since then many scientists from The Scripps Institution of Oceanography, Woods Hole Oceanographic Institution, and universities with departments of oceanography have searched for more of these vents, finding

Hot water and minerals pour from a black smoker which was found on the East Pacific Rise in 1979.

54

them in the Pacific Ocean from the East Pacific Ridge, off the coast of Peru, up to the Juan de Fuca Ridge 200 miles (400 kilometers) off the Oregon-Washington coastline. Oceanographers were surprised to find hot-spring vents in the mid-Atlantic, near the Mid-Atlantic Ridge.

Vents are found in fissures, where the earth's crust has cracked and is spreading apart at the rate of about an inch or more a year. Seawater moves down into the fissures until it contacts deep layers of hot rock. The water becomes very hot and rushes back upward, carrying minerals with it.

The first attempt to take the temperature of the water melted the thermometer, but later tests found measurements up to 650 degrees Fahrenheit (350 degrees Celsius). The water spewing through the chimneys looks like black or white smoke, because it is colored by the minerals it carries. These minerals mix with the seawater, which causes them to cool and become solids. They form chimneys around the vents. Deposits of iron, manganese, copper, zinc, lead, and silver have been found in and around the black smokers.

How Will Knowledge of the Ocean Floor Help Us?

When telephone cables were first laid across the oceans, they were often broken. After scientists had been able to discover the submarine canyons with their violent currents and avalanches, they knew how the cables had been broken. So they avoided these canyons in laying new cable and solved the problem.

The wealth of minerals already found on the sea floor is thought to be only a part of the minerals which exist under the sea. Manganese nodules found on the sea floor have been estimated at 1.5 trillion tons, a quarter of which is manganese, 1.2 percent copper, 1.5 percent nickel, and 0.2 percent cobalt. A deposit of copper cones tens of feet high, covering an area 650 feet wide (198 meters) and 3,200 feet long (975 meters), was discovered along a fracture zone in an undersea ridge 350 miles (563 kilometers) west of Ecuador. Dr. Alex Malahoff, chief scientist of the National Ocean Survey, told newspaper reporters that it may be the richest known ore anywhere in the world, perhaps worth over $2 billion. Oceanographers

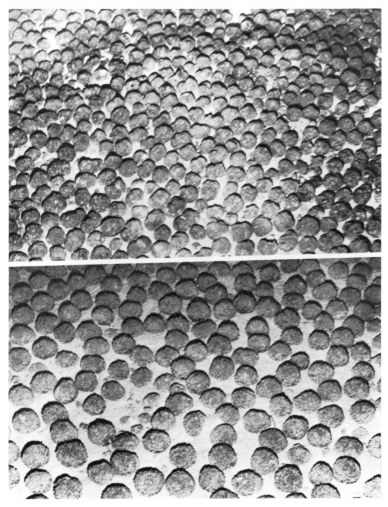

Manganese nodules cover the sea floor at a depth of 17,362 feet (5,292 meters) in the southwest Pacific Ocean. Each nodule is about 4 inches in diameter. Someday this field of manganese may be commercially mined.

57

have found large deposits of sand and gravel within 200 miles off the coasts of the United States, and these materials are needed in building construction.

Although at the present time mining at great depths below the sea would probably be too expensive to be practical, tools for underwater mining have already been invented, underwater mining companies have been formed, and countries are working to develop laws of the sea which will decide how these mineral deposits will be shared.

Geologists, in studying the continental shelves, have been able to find drilling sites for oil and gas. While many oil companies have drilled producing wells offshore, they may find new petroleum sources in even deeper waters.

As new equipment is invented and developed, new sea-floor discoveries will be made that will help us better understand the total picture of the earth and how we can best use this knowledge.

Geophysicist Dr. Hans Schouten of Woods Hole is one of the oceanographers who points out that it takes a

These are some of the offices and docks of the Woods Hole Oceanographic Institution. Many WHOI offices and laboratories are located in a nearby campus.

combination of sciences to get the answers from under the sea. The men and women who work as oceanographers are geologists, zoologists, geophysicists, biologists, paleontologists, petrologists, botanists, and chemists. At the present time these oceanographers are working in the role of pioneers, sharing their knowledge to learn more about the land found under the sea—once a mystery, now a new frontier.

INDEX